The Dance of the Dust
on the Rafters

the Dance *of the* Dust *on the* Rafters

Selections from
Ryojin-hisho

Translated by
Yasuhiko Moriguchi
and David Jenkins

Broken Moon Press

Printed in the United States of America.

ISBN 0-913089-10-9
Library of Congress Catalog Card Number: 89-61143

The cover background is from a nineteenth-century *hanten,*
or short coat, woven in *saki-ori* style (strips of discarded
or worn-out garments combined with cotton threads).
Courtesy of Marvel On Madison Asian Antiquities,
Seattle, Washington.

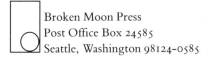
Broken Moon Press
Post Office Box 24585
Seattle, Washington 98124-0585

for John Lennon

. . . our little memories are but a part of some great Memory that renews the world and men's thoughts age after age, and . . . our thoughts are not, as we suppose, the deep, but a little foam upon the deep.

W. B. YEATS

Contents

Introduction

Ryojin-hisho, one of Japan's great masterpieces of
literary folk art, is a collection of songs of faith and
love that first appeared as an anthology in the late
twelfth century, toward the end of the Heian period
(794–1192). Centuries later, the songs still resonate
with honesty and compelling spiritual power. They
address quite directly our modern age.

The name *Ryojin-hisho* is derived from two
sources. *Ryojin* literally means "roof-beam-dust" and
it refers to a Chinese legend which tells of two singers
whose stirring performances caused the very dust on
the rafters to rise up, not to settle for three full days.
Hisho is commonly translated as "secret book," which
implies an esoteric tradition. It can be less misleadingly
given as "book of secrets," implying the truths that
are to be revealed, rather than concealed.

The precise origins of these songs—also known
as *imayo,* or "present-day style"—are unknown. One
traditional source places their origin in the sixth century,
which would mean that they may predate even the
monumental *Man'yoshu,* with which some of these
songs share a certain similarity. But this cannot,
and presumably will not, be definitely established.

What is known is that the songs were flourishing
in the capital city of Kyoto by the end of the tenth
century. They had been popularized by street enter-
tainers and were now enjoying a certain vogue
among the gentry. One of the earliest direct references

to *imayo* is contained in the diary of Lady Murasaki, author of *The Tale of Genji,* who tells of a garden party at which these and other seemingly frivolous songs were played, to everyone's great amusement. No doubt *imayo* were considered rather raffish and unseemly, but they gradually gained respectability—probably because of the high religious tone of many of them—even at court. It is to the Emperor Go-Shirakawa (1127–1192) that we owe their survival, albeit now in sadly depleted form. In his youth something of a Prince Hal, Go-Shirakawa eagerly sought the company of the *asobi*—gypsy-like strollers and players—frequently inviting them to the Imperial Palace, and assiduously collecting their songs. He amassed a collection of thousands of such songs, which he arranged in twenty volumes, with extensive notes on their style of performance and, probably, musical annotations. Today, only 566 songs—that is, the second book, with fragments of the first—remain.

We may, as is often done, divide the songs into three basic sections: Buddhist songs, folk songs, and Shinto shrine-songs. This, however, brings us very far from the mark. To the extent that some songs refer specifically to Buddhist deities or contain fragments of the sutras, they may be said to be Buddhist songs. Yet all of these songs, even the most sensual or embittered, are imbued with Buddhist values. Here, when men and women sing of their love for each other, or when a man sings of his work as a fisherman, they are singing with an eye on the beyond, with concern for the life of the soul, as protected and assured by the Buddhist religion. In addition, while the songs sometimes refer directly to certain shrines, Shinto animism—expressed in a deep reverence for nature and man's place in it—is inseparably intertwined with the overall spirit. At the same time, while some songs were adopted by the Buddhist clergy as a means to proselytize in the common people's own language, the tradition from which all of them sprang is essentially a folk tradition, particularly that of the performing arts. These three strands seamlessly form a melding which is uniquely Japanese, and which in *Ryojin-hisho* finds a consummate form.

The times from which these songs emerge were, to say the least, turbulent. It is generally thought that Go-Shirakawa had completed the main part of his collection by 1169, although he was to add more to it in succeeding years. These years are of great historical importance, as they represent a major turning-point, when the center of power (of which Go-Shirakawa himself was a dying ember) moved from the court at Kyoto and solidified in the East in Kamakura, where, after the Gempei civil war (1180–1185), the powerful Minamoto clan was to establish a military dictatorship and the basis of a feudal society that was to remain very little changed in nature for almost seven centuries.

While much is known of the rulers and of the political developments of the time, almost nothing is known of the life of the common people. But what little we do know reveals conditions—notably in Kyoto—that are little short of calamitous. From the chronicle *Hojoki,* kept by a recluse living on the outskirts of the city, we learn of poverty, of almost constant pestilence, of earthquakes, storms, and famine, of a time when men stole images of Buddha to use as firewood, of a time when infants could be seen still clutching the breasts of their dead mothers. In one two-month period, some forty-two thousand corpses were found unburied in the city.

The chronicle tells of devastating fires, the perennial scourge of the city. There is, in particular, a description of one conflagration in 1177 which destroyed one-third of Kyoto and claimed the lives of thousands of people. To this we should add the frequent mayhem visited on the city by the *yamahoshi,* the warrior "monks." These were little better than mercenary bandits hired by the great temples to protect their property—but more usually to raid that of their neighbors, under sacerdotal protection. Finally, there was the social disorder associated with the struggle between the Taira and Minamoto clans, both of which were able to field armies of unprecedented size (even allowing for the exaggerations of contemporary chronicles).

The literature of the time is generally awash in religious pessimism. The belief was common that the

age of *Mappo*—the "end of the Law"—had arrived.
This was supposed to be the final era of the Buddhistic
world, a time of chaos and the decline of morality.
It was commonly supposed to begin fifteen hundred
years after the death of Gautama Buddha, a time which
roughly corresponded to the late Heian period. At the
same time, however, there was a conviction that
deliverance was at hand, that common people might be
aided in their travails by such deities as Kannon, Jizo,
Yakushi, and, in particular, Amitabha, or Amida,
the Lord of the Western Paradise.

In light of this, *Ryojin-hisho* can be seen as tes-
timony to the remarkable ability of people to transcend
the horror of their age, indeed to transcend with
dignity, with their faculty of lovingness intact.

There is no doubt that Go-Shirakawa saw in
Ryojin-hisho the means of his own redemption. This
was a time of the introduction of feudal discipline,
and yet it was also the time of a certain religious
emancipation. So if common people could expect
salvation, then why not the emperor too? He wrote:
"I have lived for fifty-some years, and it's been as if
in a dream, like a phantom. Most of my life has now
passed. Now I would gladly throw everything away
and simply hope for paradise. If I were to sing *imayo*
now, why should I not be taken to the Lotus Seat?
Why not? For even the *asobi* and the likes of them, who
ride in boats floating on the waves, pushing against the

flow with poles, dressed in kimono, who know love, and lusting after each other . . . even they will be allowed into paradise. Why not me too?"

Go-Shirakawa was a complex, contradictory man. He was, in fact, emperor for only three years or so. Following custom, he then abdicated, to enter a cloister, from which, like his predecessors, he was able to exercise, if not power, then at least a certain indirect influence.

He was to be "Cloister Emperor" for more than thirty years, and even as the social order was crumbling around him, he remained convinced that he might yet wield real power in the land. In truth, the "power" of the emperors had long since been confined to the role of providing a source of legitimacy to a succession of powerful regents who were de facto rulers of Japan. With the decline of the Fujiwara family, who had provided regents for several hundred years and had very astutely married into the royal family, the resulting vacuum was to be filled by contesting military clans— of which the victors were to provide the first of a long succession of *Shogun,* who more or less disregarded the wishes of the emperor and sometimes treated the incumbent with contumely.

In this vacuum, Go-Shirakawa attempted to exert his influence. History's verdict on him is not altogether kind. Politically, he is considered unprincipled, a crafty schemer, a manipulator. However, the reality was that he was not so much manipulator as manipulated, much given to conspiracies which blew up in his face, switching his support from one contestant for power to another.

Yet this was a man, devious and sometimes cruel, whose real life's work was the collection of a body of poetry of great clarity and beauty that sprang from the very heart of his people.

In *Ryojin-hisho* we find a teeming world of priests and prostitutes, peasants and hunters, gamblers and gossipers, toilers and outcasts, old men and children, whose voices are sometimes interchangeable. The songs are at once lusty and devotional. Above all, they are entertainment.

One modern Japanese commentator—who subtitled a long essay on *Ryojin-hisho* "Songs of Faith and Love-lust"—has remarked: "Entertainment and faith have been folkways [in Japan] that have been the front and back of the same thing from the most ancient times." In these songs, there is a robust sense of play. All the Japanese love of word-play is here. But one song warns: "Pretty words / empty words / are our error." That is, words devoid of love are sinful. This song goes on to promise that if our words are ultimately used in praise of Buddha, then "all words / rough and smooth / go back / to their first meaning." That is, our words revert to their true place as our most treasured gift, and may themselves become great deeds.

Here is a quasi-alchemic notion of words that relates directly to the doctrine that to read any chapter of the *Lotus Sutra* just once will bring great merit, and to intone the name of Amida correctly and devotedly just once will assure the sinner of entry into paradise. This doctrine was very commonly preached at the time, and it is also occasionally directly referred to in these songs.

If almost nothing is known of the lives of the common people of the late-Heian period, even less is known of the *asobi* who strolled among them performing these songs. With the *kugutsu,* or puppeteers, they wandered the cities and the main highways and waterways, sometimes setting up stalls, and performing magic shows, telling fortunes, and singing *imayo*.

The great volume of *imayo* from which Go-Shirakawa was able to choose suggests a certain element of spontaneity. They were to lose this element of spontaneity in the Kamakura period, becoming more a stylized repertoire of popular songs. Frequently they were performed as accompaniment to dance, and in particular to the *shirabyoshi*—"white beat"— style of dance, and it has been suggested that, together, *imayo* and *shirabyoshi* are direct precursors of the *Noh* dramatic form, which itself went through a radical and mysterious stage of formalization in the early fourteenth century.

We cannot know how or when Go-Shirakawa was first drawn to these songs. Late in life he wrote: "For a long time, ever since I was in my teens, I have loved *imayo,* and have never been long without [hearing] them . . . In all seasons, any day, I would sing all day, and there was hardly a night when I didn't sing all night too . . . I used to live without thought for day or night. Days and months passed, and I would gather people round and we would dance and play and sing . . . I even lost my voice three times . . . I have strained myself so that my throat became so swollen I couldn't even drink water. But still I forced myself to sing . . . I sang with people in the court, but also invited singers from [the streets of] Kagamiyama and Kanzaki . . . I have truly loved *imayo,* and so have passed almost sixty springs and autumns."

Eventually, the day of the *imayo* was to pass, as new styles of song and dance supplanted them in the popular consciousness. It is more than likely that much of the original collection was dispersed among other collections, which themselves disappeared.

It is only in comparatively modern times, in 1911, that these songs were rediscovered in their present form. Most curiously, the bulk was discovered among a collection of old manuscripts in a used-book store in Tokyo by the historian Hidematsu Wada. They were republished in 1912 and underwent something of a revival in the early Taisho period, having considerable influence on contemporary poets. One of these, Hakushu Kitahara, spoke of a "piercing golden light" emanating from them. They have now retaken their place in the canon of classical Japanese literature, and also find a special place in the history of the development of the spirituality of all people.

Book
I

Celebration

May you live as long
as the speck of dust
that settles once
in a thousand years
then builds
into a mountain
topped
with a white cloud

(1)

Spring

I didn't think you'd come.
 You must have seen
 the plum tree
 blooming
 in my garden.

(3)

 ## Summer

In my yard
beside the pond
wisteria
      rippling in the wind like waves
has bloomed.

When will you come
      young mountain cuckoo
come and sing?

(4)

🍃 Autumn

You cannot see the autumn come
    —you hear it
        suddenly
            in the wind.

(5)

Winter

Dimly,
  in the dawning sky,
  the moon shines,
    and in its light
  the maple leaves are scattered
    by the mountain wind.

(6)

Wisteria winds around the willow,
    flowers hanging, smelling sweet.
The willow and wisteria sway,
    gently twining, playing in the wind.
The slender green willow
    gives such joy,
        such joy.

(11)

We can't quench our thirst
        from the mountain spring.
Even with the drops
        that fall from careful hands
        we cloud the pool.

So, unquenched,
        I have parted from you.

(10)

Do not pine away, my love.
    As we both must
        go on living in this world
    so must we both
        surely meet again.

(9)

Book
2

So are we born
        to sing and dance
                and laugh and play?
When I hear
        the sound of children play
                I feel my old body
                        start to move.

(359)

Pretty words
        empty words
                are   our   error.

But if
        we use words
                in praise of Buddha
                        as seeds
they say all words
        rough and smooth
                go back
                        to their first meaning.

(222)

The eyes of love
        open brightly
                like a lotus bloom.

The light of wisdom
        shines in majesty
                like the morning sun.

(223)

Even the deer
        that lives in the hills
                may become a Buddha.

It gives its hair—
neatly tied
it makes a brush
                which writes
                the teaching
                of the One Way
and thus
        it gains grace,
                even the deer.

(239)

At break of day
        when all is still
I lie there, half-awake,
            just thinking.

I can't help the tears that start.
Have I lived this life in vain?
Oh, when will I be saved?

(238)

To make a living
    in this world of dreams,
I fished in the seas
    and hunted in the hills,
so all the Buddhas now have fled from me.

Now how am I supposed to live
    the next life?

(240)

Once you see
        that all things come
                from the longings of this world
then you will know
        the fires of deepest hell
                are also of the mind.

When your heart
        becomes still and clear
                then it's really
                not so far from you
                to the water of the pond
                of paradise.

(241)

The charms of Sagano are
    the boats of cormorant fisher folk,
    the helmsmen of the rafts,
    maple leaves floating on the stream,
        the sound of the harp
        filling the air
        in the shade of the hill.
This is all so like
    a frolic
        in a pure, pure land.

(309)

Loving
loving always—
in the sky
the Weaver star,
shooting stars
and in the fields
copper pheasants
yes and then
the strollers,
mandarin ducks in winter,
love-birds all.

(334)

Here above
in heaven
as night sinks
into the darkest hours
cranes sleep
listen
listen
to the spring-water
rush rush rush.
This is
just like the world
I left behind
so see
the big wild geese
hear their shrieks
on the autumn breeze.
This is
just as it was
on earth
there below.

(227)

The realm of highest heaven
　　　is so pure, and yet
　　　　　it's not beyond
　　　　　　　the mind of common people.

The realm of deepest hell
　　　is base, and yet
　　　　　it dwells in the soul of a saint,
　　　　　　or so they say.

(214)

Your life is like
    the high sigh
        of the breeze blowing
            through the pines

and all in all
    all is well
        well being
            here among the pines
            at Sumiyoshi.

(543)

How full of wonders heaven is.
There is nothing without meaning there.
>   The wind that sighs
>   the waves that rise
>   the birds,
>   all sing the Holy Word.

(177)

How pure the coming paradise.

As the era changes,
        and we look to the end of the world,
                the moonlight,
                still and clear,
                shines
                on each and every thing.

(34)

The sea at Akashi
        strokes the sand,
                the water
                        frothing in and out,
                                fondling the beach.

Though no wind moves,
        ripples form,
                just waves making
                        baby waves.

(350)

There is
just one
paradise.

Unless you set yourself
to seeking it
then it's very far indeed.

But it's just because
our minds are dull
we think it far
when, truly
        it is near.

(175)

My thoughts of him
    are strong enough
        to reach the farthest North.

My love for him
    could stretch from here
        to the East and back.

But if we had not joined in love
    why, maybe, after all
        I might have just
        forgotten all about him.

(335)

Here at Ninomiya
　　　where the hill-stream
　　　　　is cool and clear
I have stayed
　　　and lived a monk's life
　　　　　hard and spare
　　　　　for six whole years.
I don't care
　　　if my prayer-beads wear away.
They say even one small child
　　　playing in the sand
　　　　　can reach the truth,
　　　　　so why not me too?

(268)

When as a monk
I wandered round,
I set my foot
upon Cape Suzu.
    I walked along the cape coast
    and in the end came right around,
    then travelled on alone,
        and on the Koshi road
        my foot went lame
        —how hard,
        how hard it was!

(300)

As a monk
I walked abroad,
    a robe upon my shoulder
    and a basket at my back,
    my clothes soaked through
    with salty water,
        walking always
        on the lonely coast
        of Shikoku.

(301)

While out picking herbs
in the burnt spring field
I see a hermit in his cave,
        all alone.

Better than meet like this
        out here in the fields
come along to my humble hut,
        holy hermit,
even though it is no grand place.

(302)

Demons of desire
        come to tempt
                the hermit in this lowly hut.

But when the morning star
        comes out at last
                they yield,
                        tamed.

(303)

Even though I sleep alone
        a hundred days, a hundred nights,
                I don't want another's man.

I don't want that kind of man
        so I can bear it
                from the evening
                till those darkest hours.

But at dawn
I lie and listen
to the rooster cry
        and feel the emptiness
                of this bed.

(336)

Now winter comes
    to the hills
        where we mountain monks
            live a life of prayer.

The leaves
    which gave us such fine thatch
        have yellowed, fallen,
            every one.

How desolate the sky.

The first frost falls upon the moss,
    which gave us soft soft beds,
        and now snow, too, has settled.

Even the stream
    which danced upon the rocks
        has frozen hard.

(305)

In the soundless temple-hall
　　　we offer Buddha
　　　　　flowers and incense.

We quiet our mind
　　　and read the Lotus Sutra
　　　　　for a while.

Then,
　　　and then,
　　　　　our Lord appears.

(102)

Sin is
an evening frost.

It flees
the light of love.

So you must
still your mind

and try
to see the truth.

(56)

The *Prajnaparamita*
　　　is a spring creek.

When the ice of lies melts,
　　　rapids swell
　　　　　telling you
　　　　　　　that which is / is not

　　　and reach the beach
　　　　　of pure life.

(52)

At times I sense
and seem to breathe
the haze,
        a garden full of flowers,
        midnight moon
        and autumn meadow,
love that does not care
if you are high
or lowly,
        water at the falls,
        trickling through the rocks.

(333)

I long to go to pray
at Kumano.

But if I walk, all the way
        it's very far,
            the
                hills
                    are
                        steep.

I long to go to pray
at Kumano.

But if I go by horse,
        then where's the holy suffering?

I long to go to pray
at Kumano.

Oh, let me fly there.
        Please, Nyakuoji,
        give me wings!

(258)

Who dances really nicely?
Yes,

    the priestess at the shrine,

    the little leaves of the great oak,

and then, I feel,

    the center of a wheel,

    the spinning-top,

    the midgets, clowns, and puppets,

and in the flowery garden,

    butterflies and little birds.

(330)

Now is that the way
      —*clung! clung!*—
            to ring the bells,
                  young Todamiko?

Here, shake the bells
      —*clink! clink!*—
            above your eyes,
                  up, up,
                  swing them up!

If you let them down
      —*clunk! clunk!*—
            below your eyes,
                  then God will see and say,
                  This girl is lazy!

      You'll be sorry, girl!

(324)

The drum
    the shrine-maid plays
    on Mount Yoshino
        sounds so fine
  as the sticks strike,
      up and down,
          thrumming.

    Let us also go there
             —there it goes,
            rat-tat-tat,
          there it goes—
  oh, how I wonder how
      she plays it so
      the sound stays,
         ringing in our ears,
            the drum.

(265)

In the ocean
　　　the ageless turtle plays.
On its back
　　　stand the three holy mountains,
　　　　　Horai, Hojo, Eishu.

The years of these mountains,
　　　and of the turtle bearing them,
　　　　added all together,
　　　I would wish for you.
All of that, I'd give to you.

(318)

From high,
 the moon shines on Mount Shumi.
It shines upon the water of the Lotus Pond.

There's a turtle at the waterside,
 where the Seven Gems gleam.

It's playing there,
 as eternity glides by.

(321)

Buddha is always here,
　　　yet, sad but true,
　　　　　he's nowhere to be seen.

But around the dawn,
　　　with sounds of people hushed,
　　　　　he appears,
　　　　　　　dimly, in my dreams.

(26)

What really strikes you in the autumn
    is the sound of clappers
        in the mountain fields,
    pulled to scare the deer away,
      and the lonely sound
        of a woman beating cloth.

(332)

At the Moji barrier in Tsukushi,
  the keeper of the gate is getting old.
   His hair is turning white.

Why on earth is he concerned
  to check the flow of people through the gate?

Better he should try to check the flow
  of his advancing years.

(328)

In Tsukushi
people tell me
there's a metal
they call bronze
and another
they call tin.
      Put together
      these two metals
      make a little vessel
      that
      somehow looks like pearl.
         How wondrous,
         strange.

(329)

Now this
is the rule of my hunting-lodge:
Make him stand outside your room
                    a while.

Make him learn his lesson
            while the night's still young.
(You see, last night he stayed away.)

And even if he's come to say he's sorry,
            yes, even if he repents,
                    turn your eyes away,
                        for a while.

(338)

You!

> You let me trust you—
>> now you stay away!

> May you turn
>> into a demon
>> with   three   horns!

> May everyone recoil from you!

Go!

> Be a bird in the paddies,
> in the frost and snow and hail!
>> May your feet freeeeze!

Go!

> Be a weed,
>> drifting on a pond!

Go!

> Be gone!
>> Push off!

(339)

I hear young Kaja
        came to take a wife.

He came on like a husband
        for two nights,
        then the third,
                past the darkest hour,
                his skirts tucked in,
                he
                    took
                        to
                            his
                                heels,
                off into the dawn.

(340)

You are heartless,
                heartless.

If it were I
        who said I could not stay with you,
                then, yes then, you might hate me.

But it's father and mother
        who want us to part.

Oh, cut me into little bits.
        As for me,
                I'd never say good-bye.

(341)

When I see some lovely girl,
  I long to be a vine,
    from top to toe entwined with her.

You could try to hack me down,
  but we'd be bound
    never more to come apart.

(342)

That rush hat you loved so well
                              fell
                              fell
                    into the Kamo river.

All that sweet rustling night
                    we felt
                and searched around
            until that autumn night was gone.

(343)

To Loveless Beach
    no rare rosewood
        or good red wood
           drifts near.

Only lowly bamboo
    blows over
        while the waves flow on,
           fluting.

(347)

Well now,
> here is a house with many fine steeds.
> It must be a warrior's home.

> > Look there—
> > > a small child
> > > is doing a jig
> > > on the shoulders
> > > of a dancing monk.

> > > And,
> > > you know,
> > > I do believe
> > > that shrine-maid
> > > over there
> > > really is
> > > a male dancer
> > > from Hakata.

(352)

The pet monkey
		that was kept
		in the corner
		of the stable
		has freed itself
		from its rope.
See how it plays
		climbing
		in the trees.

				On the mountain
				at Tokiwa
				the branches of the oak
				are dancing in the wind.

(353)

Do your best,
      old gray-haired man.

Follow Buddha's way,
      and lead a good life.

Even the cranes in the valley,
      gray-haired too,
            live a thousand years.

(354)

What wretched creatures
    we who fish with cormorants are!

I have killed the turtles
    which were meant to live a thousand years,
        and bound my birds' throats.

I may go on living in this way
    in this world
        —but how will I live through the next?

(355)

Do you mean to say
    that after visiting this shrine
        I must go home
           without a little change of scene?

Even the deer that lives in the hills
    must change the color of his hide
        from summertime to winter.

(360)

I left my home in Kai
    and staggered
        over Misaka Pass in Shinano,
          all the way here.

Not that I'm some baby chick,
    but how can I go home again,
        with fluff
          still on my chin?

(361)

The young tufts
of bamboo grass
stay nice and thick,
even though
the horses nibble.
        In my bedroom,
        even though you never come,
        my bed is never empty,
        for I too am young.

(362)

I only have
a girl and boy.

My girl was wanted
in the kitchen
of a lord in Kyoto
so I've given her away.

My boy was wanted
as a sailor
on the fast boat
of a priest
of a big country shrine
so I've given him away too.

Look down on me
you gods and Buddhas.
       Why have you cursed me so,
       great Wakamiya?

(363)

I suppose
my girl is over ten now,
  wandering with the strollers.

When she walks on Tago beach
the fishermen come pressing round
and say to her
  "Hey, child! that fortune's right!"
and play around with her,
  poor love.

(364)

My son is maybe twenty now,
but round the land he goes,
           a gambling man, a gambling man.
Lord help him.
Please don't let him lose.
For even though he runs around,
           gambling here, gambling there,
I can't get angry—
           he's my boy.

(365)

Let me tell you
how my children are.

The eldest
is a gambler
always losing
never winning.

The next
is in a temple,
though still young,
and loves
to play around
at night.

My girl?
My girl is just a slut.

What a pain it is.

(366)

The old Yamashiro eggplant
            now is over-ripe.
I've left her on the vine too long
            —she's gone all red.
Should I throw her out?

Aw no, let's keep her,
            let's at least get seed from her.

(372)

Things that bow before the wind are
     the top-most branches
     of the pine,
     bamboo fronds,
          and out at sea
     ships,
     their sails hoisted high,
          while in the sky
     clouds,
          then, in the fields
     the very tips
     of the pampas grass.

(373)

Things that are especially fleet are
        the falcon and the peregrine,
                the great hawk
                flying from the hand
                of the hunter,
        waterfalls,
                bundles of firewood
                tumbling down the hill,
        and the answers
        to your prayers
        to the gods
        Sansho and Gosho.

(374)

They are letting my young man go
        back, back to the city
            so he's going.

We have lived
        in a house we built
            by the island cove.

But now without a backward glance
            he's leaving.

Where have I gone wrong with you,
            great god Hyakudaifu?

Why do you let him go?

(375)

Even though
he works
with common clay
the potter at Kuzuha
has a lovely daughter,
        a true beauty.
We'd like
to see this woman
carried in the grandest palanquin
in a train
of three or four
and have her called
        the governor's wife.

(376)

Though as you see
I'm dressed for now
in this poor way
in fact my uncle
is the priest Ichiman
          of Daianji.
I've a fine nephew too
and my son studies
          at Todaiji.

It's just because
it looked like rain
          I came without
          my finer clothes.

(377)

What the stroller really wants
is a song to sing, a drum to tap,
a little boat, a little shade,
some smiling woman rowing her,
and
              —Hyakudaifu! god of the road—
                      the loving of a man.

(380)

In this world, what I can't stand
     is the sight of a priest on a prancing pony,
         rearing, whinnying to the wind,
     is an old man with gray hair
         running after young girls,
     is a jealous mother
         got up like a nun.

(384)

The wood-choppers
on their way
to Nishiyama
now are crossing
Katsura river,
        all in a line.

        Is the fellow
        at the back
        new to this game?

                He's been toppled
                by the waves,
                he's thrown
                his resting-stick down
                and now he flounders
                in the flowing foam.

(385)

The crow is black,
　　the heron white,
　　even with the passing of the years.

The neck of the duck
　　　　　is short.
　　What is there
　　　　that I can add?

The legs of the crane
　　　　　are long.
　　What is there
　　　　that I can take away?

(386)

If you go west of the city
    you will find the pretty
        love-birds,
              sparrows, swallows, cuckoos,
            so I hear.

There are so many men these days
    who love the pleasures of the bed,
        but you don't mind
           if I don't do so,
              do you, dear?

(388)

There go the bulls,
      the famous bulls of Awaji,
            across the water, horns in line.

The cows come after,
      and behind,
            the bullocks that they bore.

Now there trot
      some baby calves,
            all with spotted backs.

(390)

Things that bend—
       prawns,
           gins,
                horns of cows,
           tips of crowns,
        spines of old men
    on canes.

(391)

Under a little
thorny
bush

a
weasel
plays
the
flute

a monkey dances

while a locust looks on
clapping

and the cricket,
well, the cricket
is the king
of tambourine.

(392)

It moves the heart to see
    a tumbledown shrine
        in a lonely field
        without a priest
        or anyone attending it,
            crumbling down,
        and an old old woman
            who served so well for many years
            but never bore a child.

(397)

How I fear the fire-god.
His look is one of fury.

In one hand he holds a sword
        and in the other a rope.

Behind him the flames mount
        while in front
                he bears a frown
                        to fend off every demon.

(284)

How I fear the woodsman.
His looks are wild and woolly.

In one hand he holds a scythe
        and in the other an axe.

Behind him the wood mounts
        while in front
                he bears a staff
                        to fend off every ranger.

(399)

There is fine music
by the sea.
        The pines
        in the wood by the beach
        sound like a harp
        while waves come drumming in
                and fish-hawks and plovers
                dance and swoop and play.

(400)

The gods
my neighbor's eldest daughter
celebrates are
      curly hair
      unruly hair
      hair that falls
      upon the brow.

On her fingers
lives the god of
      "I'm all thumbs"
and on her toes
there lives the god of
      tripping round.

(402)

There are, I know,
so many waterfalls
but for now
how good it is to hear the sound
of this one.

Even though the sun is burning down
It just keeps rushing
                    rushing.

(404)

Dance   dance
        dance   dance
   Little   little
        snail   snail.

If you don't
            dance dance,
            little snail,
I will give you to a horsey,
    to a horsey
                or a moo-cow,
and they'll stomp you with their feet
            (stomp-stomp! splat-splat!).

            But,

    if you dance
                pretty-pretty,
I will take you to a garden,
        and you'll play and play
            all day.

(408)

As the mirror darkens
      so I see my face is getting lined.
As my face gets to be lined,
      well then
      the men
         will stay away.

(409)

A little louse is playing in my hair.
He likes to head
        for the scruff of my neck
            to eat.
But in the end
                from the teeth
                of a comb,
        he comes down from high

                to
                the
                bucket-
                lid,

                    and there
                    his life
                    is snuffed
                    out.

(410)

I don't want to be a hermit.

I wouldn't like to wear the robe
                    and carry beads.

I just want to play
                    and frolic, now,
                    while I'm young.

(426)

The things you find around
        those frightful mountain-monks
        —such tasteless things!—
            are
        dried-out frozen yams,
                    horseradish,
            plain rice offered to the Lord,
        drops of water,
                    roots of parsley
                    that grows way down
                        in the valley.

(427)

I tell you what is glum—
a road at night,
boat-trips,
a traveller's way,
wayside inns,
the chanting of a sutra
from a mountain temple
in the darkness
of a looming forest,
the sad sad parting
of a couple
still in love.

(429)

At Matsuyama in Sanuki
    a crooked pine,
        bent and twisted,
          seething,
            writhing.

They have planted it again
    at Naoshima but
        why don't they try
          to make that plain old pine
           straight?

(431)

Lovely things in early spring—
  the haze,
    bush warblers,
      wild geese flying home,
  the first Day of the Rat,
    green willows,
      plum and cherry blossom,
  and
  the peach-tree they say bears fruit
    once
      every three thousand years.

(432)

I stopped
in the shade of a pine
and while I lapped the water
pattering on the rocks
I thought no more of taking up my fan.

I felt it was a year without a summer.

(433)

At the edge of the pond
    where it's really cool
        there is no sign of summer.

The sound of the breeze
    that blows high up
        among the tall pines—
            the sound of autumn.

(434)

Wait, wait,
                    dragonfly.
Let me salt your tail.

Stay, stay,
                    dragonfly.

I'll twine you in a horse-tail hair,
and tie you to a bamboo stick
so little boys can play with you,
                                twirling.

(438)

—Come,
    my little spinning-top,
        let's go to see the fair
        at Jonanji, in Toba.

—Oh, no,
    I'm too afraid to go.
    I won't go there any more,
    for on that new road,
    at the crossing of the way,
        there are so many bad-
            tempered, stamping horses.

(439)

Oh! the moon!

    It comes back young, every month,
      while I am getting older,
        running out of life.

    How can this be?

(449)

The moon is a ship,
       the stars white-topped waves,
           and the clouds the sea.

But how can
       the man in the moon row?
           He's all alone.

(450)

In the spring field
    a young fern stands
        looking like a door-latch,
    just as if there were a hut behind.

Stand there quietly,
    young one.
Don't let just anyone raise you,
        and steal in.

(451)

Over the hedge
I see a little wild pink
I never tire of watching.

Please, wind,
blow her over here,
her roots and leaves
intact.

(452)

I thought to ask
the wind that blows
to bring my message to you.
But then again,
        it might just

                fall
            into some distant meadow.

(455)

If you love me, please
      come quickly
            quickly.
Where I live
      is at the foot of Miwayama.
You'll know it
      by the cedar at the gate.

(456)

Hear me, waves
    speak, beach
        look on, pines.

If there comes a breeze that says,
    "You,
    you,
    you're the one
        the one for me,"
    then I'll gladly
        let myself be blown
           up to any shore.

(457)

On Suma Beach
    there are nets
        spread out to dry.
But they don't catch my eye
    now that I have seen you
        and,
            caught from that first sight,
                love you.

(458)

Yesterday
     he didn't come.
     Nor the day before.
     If I don't hear from him
today,
     what shall I do
     with the time,
tomorrow?

(459)

I've loved him,
        loved him.

The rare nights we meet,
            what is the dream?

        Yes,
            reaching,
                    reaching,
            clutching,
                    clutching.

(460)

As food to calm my morning-sickness
    let me have some oysters,
        the kind you find near the beach
        at Nagato Bay,
           stuck to a rock.

Then I will bear a baby boy
    who will read and write so well,
        and like Buddha
           have the eighty holy marks
            and purple-golden skin.

(461)

In the sea at Ise
	women dive
		and gather abalone.

The love I have
	is like those abalone-shells
		—just one side.

(462)

The plain bower
    has no eaves
        joining at the crest.

Since after all
    I may not share his roof,
        why did we
        from the very start
        join breast to breast?

(464)

Takasago strand
  —"tall sand"—
      should be high but
          we see, of course, it's not.

Then, Mount Hira
  —"flat land"—
      is, in fact,
          not flat at all—
                it's   tall
                      tall
                        tall.

(466)

It rains.

"Go away," they say
to me, with no rain-hat,
          no rain-coat
          of straw.

What cold-hearted country-folk
          who won't let me stay!

(467)

The conch-shell
        the mountain-monk had on his belt
        has dropped and smashed,
        as my heart is shattered
                by this love.

(468)

The clothes
     some humble man has hung
         upon a bamboo pole
            have not yet dried.

It's been a week and
     they're still not dry,
         I wonder wonder why.

(469)

What a spooky place this is,
        high in the hills,
        deep in the woods,
        no sound of birds.

Now—
        the sound of a man!

Ah, how blessed,
        here he comes
                —a mountain-monk!

(470)

The sound of a drum
    wakes people sleeping in the night.

How tired and heavy
    the hand that beats.

My heart goes out
    to that drummer-girl.

(471)

I just arrived
        from the east
                yesterday,
                        so I have no wife yet.

Can I trade
        this fine blue cloak I'm wearing
                for a nice young girl?

(473)

In the Yodo River,
    down near the bed,
        where the water runs deep,
    there's a baby trout
        whose back is being eaten
        by a cormorant.
    It writhes and writhes—
        I feel that pain.

(475)

The waves
　　are coming in, going out,
　　advancing up the sand
　　　　before the shrine,
　　　　as if to promise
　　　　the advancement
　　　　of my master,
　　　　rising always rising,
　　　　　　the waves.

(477)

What is my master like?

Let's say he's like
     an ageless pine
     that grows
          upon a rocky ridge
          along the mountain
          on the back
          of the turtle
          off the coast.

(479)

Come,
let's love again,
just one more time.

The night is gone—
                    there's the bell.
We've loved since evening.

What shall we do
                    with this hunger!

(481)

That man
>   that fine young man
>   who serves the Lord Harima
>   I want
>   I want to have
>   I want to have him
>   have him
>   give me
>   a dress
>   dyed deep blue,
>   the kind
>   the kind they make in Shikama.

(482)

If you really want to bind a thing
        there is nothing
                that cannot be bound.

When the wind blows
        there is nothing
                that does not bend.

(484)

I love
I love you
    long for you
      to meet you
        see you
        look on you and
        have you
          look on me.

(485)

I can't resist
no, can't resist
the tempting of
    a cup of wine
    a fresh trout our cormorant caught
    a sweet young woman.
        Come along
        then
        let us
        get us
        into bed.

(487)

Clearly,
>   that's a horse
>   eating summer grass
>   by the bush.
Yes,
>   but if that were
>   an autumn field,
>   you would see a deer,
clearly.

(488)

Waves of age
        are crashing in
                to that shore
                        they call the Brow.

How I long
        for the beach
                they give the name
                        of Youth.

(490)

As night sinks
    into pitch black,
        goblins walk abroad.

Holy Lord,
    I believe,
        Holy Lord,
            I believe!

(491)

Kannon,
⠀⠀⠀her light soft,
⠀⠀⠀⠀⠀⠀stands astride
⠀⠀⠀⠀⠀⠀⠀⠀⠀the six roads of delusion
⠀⠀⠀⠀⠀⠀so that we,
⠀⠀⠀⠀⠀⠀⠀⠀⠀ever born, re-born
⠀⠀⠀⠀⠀⠀⠀⠀⠀in the three worlds of unknowing
⠀⠀⠀⠀⠀⠀⠀⠀⠀⠀⠀⠀may not be lost.

(38)

Those who do not chant
    the name of the Lord Amida
        are like rocks
            in deep deep water.

Even though the aeons pass
    there is no chance
        that they will float up.

(494)

Holy Amida
I pray,
my hands joined
to yours
by a thread,
let me end this life
with mind composed.

(493)

I am sorry
　　　　for the three flocks of sparrows
　　　　　　　at Inari shrine
for by day they play
　　　　lovingly together
then by night
　　　　they sleep alone.

(514)

It seems to me
        the gods of Inari
                have been cruel.

I know I did not pray
        for someone else
                to have you.

(520)

Does God not also
        enjoy for today
            the eight superb
                dancing-girls
                    at Kasuga?

(523)

At Sumiyoshi
　　　　a shrine-maid dances
　　　　　　at the outer gate,
　　　　　　　　a god within her.

She wears a wig
　　　　and a borrowed dancing frock,
　　　　　　its hem frayed
　　　　　　　　at the back.

(545)

If you are a true god,
      come down,
            possess this maiden,
                 rustling, stirring her.

Whoever heard
          of a shy god?

(559)

What kind of shaman is this?
Her unlined skirt hitched up
    to show her arse
        the woman seems possessed
           gabbling out the oracle.
Just look at this,
        why don't you?

(560)

Iwashimizu—

    I am bound to
    where this water goes
    for I am worthless
    flotsam
        bobbing in the flow.

(499)

With these thousand pines
    the thousand pines of Ohmi woods
        I would give you
           give you life
                that lasts
                    a full thousand years.

(563)

How glad I am to live
in a world of peace
as timeless as
this flowing stream
at Iwashimizu.

(498)

Oh, you Buddhas
    who have reached
    the highest light,
        bless me
        with your secret help
        as I stand here
        in this wooded field.

(565)

I always thought
        I'd pick a posy,
                just for you.
Now, here I am
        picking
        picking plants to offer
        at a service
                for your soul.

(566)

About the Translators

Yasuhiko Moriguchi and David Jenkins live in Kyoto, Japan, where they are language teachers. Yasuhiko Moriguchi was born in Yoshino, in Nara Prefecture. He was educated in Nara and in Missouri, where he received his bachelor's degree in philosophy. David Jenkins grew up in the northeast of England. He worked for several years as a journalist and editor in London and in the United States. They have been collaborating since 1981, and are now at work translating the *Kanginshu,* the sixteenth-century collection of *kouta,* or short songs.

Book design by Ken Sánchez.
Text set in Bembo on a Linotron 202
by Wilsted & Taylor, Oakland, California.
Printed on acid-free paper and Smyth sewn
by Malloy Lithographing, Inc., Ann Arbor, Michigan.